THE
COLORING
BOOK
FOR GROWN UPS

THE
COLORING
BOOK
FOR GROWN UPS

ARCTURUS

ARCTURUS

This edition published in 2015 by Arcturus Publishing Limited
26/27 Bickels Yard, 151–153 Bermondsey Street,
London SE1 3HA

ISBN: 978-1-78599-044-1
AD004884NT

Printed in China

INTRODUCTION

This bumper book will keep you absorbed for hours of coloring fun. It contains a wealth of images, from flowers to fairies and fantasy figures, for you to customize with colored pencils and make your own.

Coloring is the new yoga—but you don't have to tie yourself up in knots to get satisfying results. Taking part in this gentle form of exercise will ease your mind and give you a sense of achievement and wellbeing. You don't need to be an artist to take part in this stress-busting activity, you just have to set aside a little time. Nor do you need expensive art supplies; just a set of colored pencils or pens will do the job.

Your choice of materials depends on the type of results you want to achieve. Wax/oil-based pencils come in a wide range of colors, hardness, and types, and will give a strong, impactful result. Water-based pencils are good for delicate shading; or you might fancy using pastels, which can be blended on the page for a subtle effect.

You may prefer to use pens rather than pencils, in which case felt-tips are available in a wide range of colors and tip fineness. More detailed results can be achieved with fine liner pens, though the range of colors is more limited.

Most importantly, explore, experiment, and have fun. There are no hard and fast rules, so let creativity guide your hand and unlock a stunning world of color and happy contemplation.

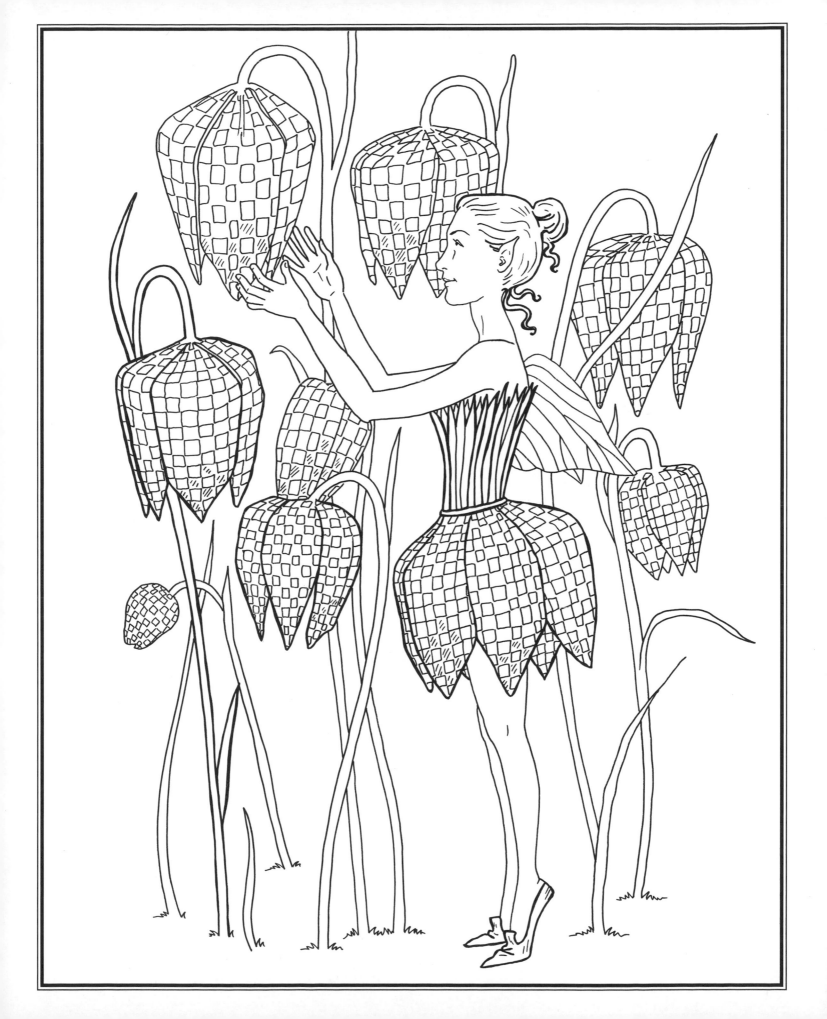

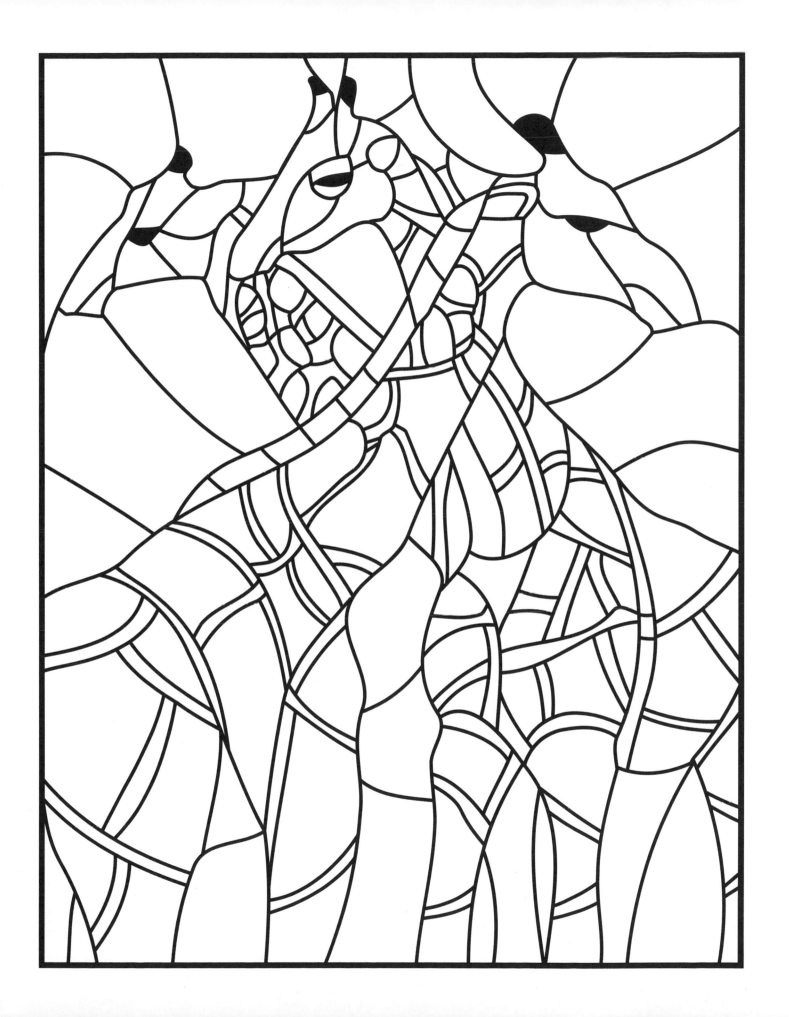